the Rottweiler

A guide to selection, care, nutrition,

upbringing, training, health, breeding,

sports and play

Contents

Foreword

The book you are holding is a basic 'owners' manual'
for everyone owning a Rottweiler and also for those
who are considering buying a Rottweiler. What we
have done in this book is to give the information to
help the (future) owner of a Rottweiler look after his
or her pet responsibly. Too many people still buy a
pet before really understanding what they're about
to get into.

This book goes into the broad history of the Rottweiler,
the breed standard and some pros and cons of buying a
Rottweiler. You will also find essential information
on feeding, initial training and an introduction in
reproduction. Finally we give attention to (day-to-day)
care, health and some breed-specific ailments.

Based on this information, you can buy a Rottweiler,
having thought it through carefully, and keep it as a pet
in a responsible manner. Our advice, though, is not just
to leave it to this small book. A properly brought-up
and well-trained dog is more than just a dog. Invest a
little extra in a puppy training course or an obedience
course. There are also excellent books available that go
deeper into certain aspects than is possible here.

About Pets

about pets

A Publication of About Pets.

co-publisher United Kingdom
Kingdom Books
PO9 5TL, England

ISBN 1852791969
First printing: September 2003
Second printing: May 2004
Third printing: June 2005

Original title: *de Rottweiler*
© 1999 - 2005 Welzo Media Productions bv,
About Pets bv
Warffum, the Netherlands
www.aboutpets.info

Photos:
Rob Doolaard, Rob Dekker,
Jos Geerts, Kingdom Books WMP,
F.A. Schaaf and D.B. de Vries

Printed in China through Printworks Int. Ltd.

In general

'The Rottweiler is not a dog for everybody.' This slogan has been applied to the Rottweiler for many years. Perhaps it's not the most appealing advertising for the breed but it is well justified.

The Rottweiler is a dog with a very specific and not always easy character. Its character coupled with its powerful body demands an owner with authority.

History

Like all dog breeds, the Rottweiler is surrounded by countless interesting theories about its origins and family history. The following story appears the most likely: In the time when the Roman empire began to extend to the North, the Roman legions marched across the Alps. The soldiers took herds of cattle with them to provide their own food. Large mastiff-type dogs herded and guarded the cattle. These heavy dogs were probably from Asia, and they were given the collective name 'Molosser'.

Apart from being used to herd cattle, these dogs were also used as fighting animals (against wild animals, people and other dogs). Some of the dogs that had accompanied the legions to Northern Europe stayed behind because they were sick or had strayed. They were also left behind as the herds began to dwindle and there was no more work for them. They often also 'established themselves' in Roman settlements. The German town of Rottweil is built on the remains of such a Roman army base. The name of Rottweil came from the words 'wil', meaning a Roman settlement, and 'rote' (red) describing the colour of the roofs. Rottweil became an important trading town in the Middle Ages because of its convenient crossroads location. Cattle traders drove their herds to the market from all around. The descendants of the Roman dogs, that had since mixed with native dogs, had a clear task: driving and guarding the cattle. At the end of the market they then had to guard their boss and his purse; there were any number of highwaymen lying in wait along the dark roads. Stories tell of the purse being bound to the dog's back and the dog then being sent home on its own.

As Rottweil's significance as a trading town diminished, the dogs became unemployed and the Rottweiler breed was threatened with extinction. However, at the beginning of the last century, the breed was rescued by the establishment of two pedigree registers: The

"Deutscher Rottweiler Klub" (German Rottweiler Club) and the "Süddeutscher Rottweiler Klub" (South German Rottweiler Club). In 1921 both clubs merged into the "Allgemeiner Deutscher Rottweiler Klub" (United German Rottweiler Club).

Character

The Rottweiler is more than just a medium-sized dog with a powerful appearance. It is very clever, exceptionally affectionate, hard-working, obedient and incorruptible. This dog has a powerful body and enormous endurance. It won't quickly become nervous.

Because of its healthy intellect and even nature, the Rottweiler is an outstanding guard dog and a fine companion for man. It is also

friendly towards other pets and a good playmate for children.

At work, the Rottweiler is totally loyal: it is well aware of the difference between work and freedom! This dog can jump, swim and climb like a champion. It is loyal, learns quickly and obeys without difficulty but, however quiet it may be, it must never be timid. A Rottweiler is a real yard dog but will not be happy on a chain. It can happily be kept outdoors all year round as long as it has shade and fresh drinking water available.

Since the first Rottweiler pedigree registers were established, the breed's characteristics have remained practically unchanged. Of great importance here is the description of the desired character. The breed associations therefore try to keep the Rottweiler's character as pure as possible by having potential breeding dogs subjected to behaviour tests. Dogs that do not meet the strict requirements of this test must not be used for breeding.

Appearance

Perhaps not everybody finds the Rottweiler pretty, but no-one can deny that it is imposing. Its powerful, somewhat more than medium-sized body, its broad head, its coarse short hair and its fine teeth give it a striking appearance. One risk in recent years is that this dog is becoming "too pretty". Its stubby hair is being replaced by a finer, smoother coat without an undercoat. This looks attractive, but is not correct. Rottweilers are also tending to become smaller and finer in build with splendid lineation. This is also not as it should be. The strict selection of dogs free of hip dysplasia (HD) has possibly played a role here. Strict selection for one point will always result in negative consequences for other points. HD is a hereditary condition of the hips that larger, heavy dogs are particularly vulnerable to. You can read more about it in the chapter Your Rottweiler's Health.

Another point deserving attention is the head. The Rottweiler needs to be a very strong dog with a very powerful head and snout. This is sometimes lacking, although it is very important to the overall picture of the dog.

Breed standard

A standard has been developed for all breeds recognised by the Kennel Club for the UK (and in Europe by the F.C.I. - the umbrella organisation for Western European kennel clubs). Officially approved kennel clubs in the member countries provide a translation. This standard provides a guideline for breeders and judges. It is something of an ideal that dogs of the breed must strive to match. With some breeds, dogs are already bred that match the ideal. Other breeds have a long way to go. There is a list of defects for each breed. These can be serious defects that disqualify the dog, and it will be excluded from breeding. Permitted defects are not serious, but do cost points in a show.

The UK Kennel Club breed standard for the Rottweiler

General Appearance
Above average size, stalwart dog. Correctly proportioned, compact and powerful form, permitting great strength, manoeuvrability and endurance.

Characteristics
Appearance displays boldness and courage. Self-assured and fearless. Calm gaze should indicate good humour.

Temperament
Good natured, not nervous, aggressive or vicious; courageous, biddable, with natural guarding instincts.

Head and Skull
Head medium length, skull broad between ears. Forehead moderately arched as seen from side. Occipital bone well developed but not conspicuous. Cheeks well boned and muscled but not prominent. Skin on head not loose, although it may form a moderate wrinkle when attentive. Muzzle fairly deep with topline level, and length of muzzle in relation to distance from well defined stop to occiput to be as 2 to 3. Nose well developed with proportionately large nostrils, always black.

Eyes
Medium size, almond-shaped, dark brown in colour, light eye undesirable, eyelids close fitting.

Ears
Pendant, small in proportion rather than large, set high and wide apart, lying flat and close to cheek.

Mouth
Teeth strong, complete dentition with scissor bite, i.e. upper teeth closely overlapping lower teeth

and set square to the jaws. Flews black and firm, falling gradually away towards corners of mouth, which do not protrude excessively.

Neck
Of fair length, strong, round and very muscular. Slightly arched, free from throatiness.

Forequarters
Shoulders well laid back, long and sloping, elbows well let down, but not loose. Legs straight, muscular, with plenty of bone and substance.

Pasterns sloping slightly forward.

Body
Chest roomy, broad and deep with well sprung ribs. Depth of brisket will not be more, and not much less than 50 per cent of shoulder height. Back straight, strong and not too long, ratio of shoulder height to length of body should be as 9 is to 10, loins short, strong and deep, flanks not tucked up. Croup of proportionate length, and broad, very slightly sloping.

Hindquarters
Upper thigh not too short, broad and strongly muscled. Lower thigh well muscled at top, strong and sinewy below. Stifles fairly well bent. Hocks well angulated without exaggeration, metatarsals not completely vertical. Strength and soundness of hock highly desirable.

Feet
Strong, round and compact with toes well arched. Hindfeet somewhat longer than front. Pads very hard, toenails short, dark and strong. Rear dewclaws removed.

Tail
Customarily docked.
Docked: Docked at first joint. Strong and not set too low. Normally carried horizontally but slightly above horizontal when dog is alert.
Undocked: Strong and not set too low. Normally carried horizontally but slightly above horizontal when dog is alert. May hang when dog is at rest.

Gait/Movement
Conveys an impression of supple strength, endurance and purpose. While back remains firm and stable there is a powerful hindthrust and good stride. First and foremost, movement should be harmonious, positive and unrestricted.

Coat

Consists of top coat and undercoat. Top coat is of medium length, coarse and flat. Undercoat, essential on the neck and thighs, should not show through top coat. Hair may also be a little longer on the back of the forelegs and breechings. Long or excessively wavy coat highly undesirable.

Colour

Black with clearly defined markings as follows: a spot over each eye, on cheeks, as a strip around each side of muzzle, but not on bridge of nose, on throat, two clear triangles on either side of the breast bone, on forelegs from carpus downward to toes, on inside of rear legs from hock to toes, but not completely eliminating black from back of legs, under tail. Colour of markings from rich tan to mahogany and should not exceed 10 per cent of body colour. White marking is highly undesirable. Black pencil markings on toes are desirable. Undercoat is grey, fawn, or black.

Size
Dogs' height at shoulder: between 63-69 cms (25-27 ins); bitches' between 58-64 cms (23-25 ins). Height should always be considered in relation to general appearance.

Faults
Any departure from the foregoing points should be considered a fault and the seriousness with which the fault should be regarded should be in exact proportion to its degree and its effect upon the health and welfare of the dog.

Note
Male animals should have two apparently normal testicles fully descended into the scrotum.

Breed standard by courtesy of the Kennel Club of Great Britain.

Critical notes on the standard:
The points required in the breed
standard are not always compatible
with the goals of a working dog.
For example, the shortening of the
snout can cause breathing difficulties
under exertion or at high tempera-
tures. In biological terms, the
optimum length of the snout is the
same or slightly longer than the
length of the skull. A short snout
also often comes with an incomplete
set of teeth, which would exclude a
Rottweiler from breeding.

A squat head with a round skull
can lead to looser skin around the
head and round protruding eyes,
whereby ectropion and entropion
arise more frequently, as well as
the occurrence of dewlaps in the
skin around the throat. The
mandatory almond-shaped eyes
with close fitting eyelids and tight
skin around the head without
dewlaps are thus, biologically
spoken, in contradiction to the
mandatory round skull.

A broad chest brings no advantages
in terms of endurance or
nimbleness and is accompanied by
a somewhat loose shoulder. A
broad chest does however promote
stability and defence in a fight,
but the loose fitting shoulder can
more easily lead to lameness. The
standard demands rough, heavy
bones, but heavy bones are less
robust than somewhat harder and
finer bones. They are also more
vulnerable to hereditary cartilage
deformities and rachitis.

These remarks may appear to
mean that show qualities alone are
not sacred. A healthy, happy dog
with good endurance is worth its
weight in gold to its master, even
if its head is a little too light, its
chest on the narrow side and its
bones a little too fine.

Buying a Rottweiler

Once you've made that properly considered decision to buy a dog, there are several options. Should it be a puppy, an adult dog, or even an older dog? Should it be a bitch or dog, a pedigree dog or a cross?

Of course, the question also comes up as to where to buy your dog - from a private person, a reliable breeder or an animal shelter? For you and the animal, it's vital to get these questions sorted out in advance. You want a dog that will suit your circumstances properly. With a puppy, you get a playful energetic housemate that will easily adapt to a new environment. If you want something quieter, an older dog is a good choice.

The pros and cons of the Rottweiler

As we said before, the Rottweiler is not an 'everybody's dog'. If you're thinking of buying a Rottweiler you must consider whether you are willing and able to give your dog a lot of time and attention. A Rottweiler needs a master with a certain psychological dominance: very consistent, without being harsh and rough. You must treat your dog as a friend, but at certain times you must be able to make it very clear that you're the boss. A Rottweiler is a working dog through and through. That work does not always mean driving cattle. A police dog training, an obedience and behaviour course or guarding its home are all meaningful tasks for this dog.

The most important thing is that you stay busy with your dog. A Rottweiler will not be satisfied with a daily walk in the woods or an hour playing with the neighbours' dogs – it needs to earn its living. Take the strong defensive traits of the Rottweiler into account: if your children are in playful combat with their friends, your dog will certainly want to defend them. If your best friend slaps you heartily on your back, he might well wind up with his arm in pain. The dog reacts this way because it perceived a threat. As soon as the danger has passed, its friendly side dominates again. All in all, a well brought-up Rottweiler that can work off its energy sufficiently is a loyal, quiet and watchful companion, which will calmly go its own way and not quickly get out of balance.

Male or female?

Whether you choose a male or a female puppy, or an adult dog or bitch, is an entirely personal decision. A male typically needs more leadership because he tends to be more dominant by nature. He will try to play boss over other dogs and, if he gets the chance, over people too. In the wild, the most dominant dog (or wolf) is always the leader of the pack. In many cases this is a male. A bitch is much more focussed on her master, she sees him as the pack leader.

A puppy test is good for defining the kind of character a young dog will develop. During a test one usually sees that a dog is more dominant than a bitch. You can often quickly recognise the bossy, the adventurous and the cautious characters. So visit the litter a couple of times early on. Try to pick a puppy that suits your own personality. A dominant dog, for instance, needs a strong hand. It will often try to see how far it can go. You must regularly make it clear who's the boss, and that it must obey all the members of the family.

When bitches are sexually mature, they will go into season. On average, a bitch is in season twice a year for about two or three weeks. This is the fertile period when she can become pregnant. Particularly in the second half of her season, she will want to go looking for a dog to mate with. A male dog will show more masculine traits once he is sexually mature. He will make sure other dogs know what territory is his by urinating as often as possible in as many places as he can. He is also difficult to restrain if there's a bitch in season nearby. As far as normal care is concerned there is little difference between a dog and a bitch.

Puppy or adult?

After you've made the decision for a male or female, the next question comes up. Should it be a puppy or an adult dog? Your household circumstances usually play a major role here.

Of course, it's great having a sweet little puppy in the house, but bringing up a young dog

requires a lot of time. In the first year of its life it learns more than during the rest of its life. This is the period when the foundations are laid for elementary matters such as house-training, obedience and social behaviour. You must reckon with the fact that your puppy will keep you busy for a couple of hours a day, certainly in the first few months. You won't need so much time with a grown dog. It has already been brought up, but this doesn't mean it won't need correcting from time to time.

A puppy will no doubt leave a trail of destruction in its wake for the first few months. With a little bad luck, this will cost you a number of rolls of wallpaper, some good shoes and a few socks.

In the worst case you'll be left with some chewed furniture. Some puppies even manage to tear curtains from their rails. With good upbringing this 'vandalism' will quickly disappear, but you won't have to worry about this if you get an older dog.

The greatest advantage of a puppy, of course, is that you can bring it up your own way. And the upbringing a dog gets (or doesn't get) is a major influence on its whole character. Finally, financial aspects may play a role in your choice. A puppy is generally (much) more expensive than an adult dog, not only in purchase price but also in 'maintenance'. A puppy needs to go to the vet's more often for the necessary

vaccinations and check-ups. Overall, bringing up a puppy involves a good deal of energy, time and money, but you have its upbringing in your own hands. An adult dog costs less money and time, but its character is already formed. You should also try to find out about the background of an adult dog. Its previous owner may have formed its character in somewhat less positive ways.

Two dogs?

Having two or more dogs in the house is not just nice for us, but also for the animals themselves. Dogs get a lot of pleasure from their own company. After all, they are pack animals.

If you're sure that you want two young dogs, it's best not to buy them at the same time. Bringing a dog up and establishing the bond between dog and master takes time, and you need to give a lot of attention to your dog in this phase. Having two puppies in the house means you have to divide your attention between them. Apart from that, there's a danger that they will focus on one another rather than on their master. Buy the second pup when the first is (almost) an adult.

Two adult dogs can happily be brought into the home together, as long as they're used to each other. If this is not the case, then they have to go through that process. This is usually best achieved by

letting them get to know each other on neutral territory. This prevents fights for territory. On neutral territory, perhaps an acquaintance's garden where neither dog has been before, both dogs are basically equal. Once they've got to know each other, you can take them both home, and they can sort out the hierarchy there amongst themselves. In any event, don't get involved in trying to 'arbitrate'. That is human, but for the dog that's at the top of the pecking order it's like having its position undone. It will only make the dog more dominant in behaviour, with all the consequences. Once the hierarchy is established, most dogs can get along fine together.

Getting a puppy when the first dog is somewhat older often has a positive effect on the older dog. The influence of the puppy almost seems to give it a second childhood. The older dog, if it's been well brought up, can help with the up-bringing of the puppy. Young dogs like to imitate the behaviour of their elders. Don't forget to give both dogs the same amount of attention. Take both out alone at least once per day during the first eighteen months. Give the older dog enough opportunity to get some peace and quiet. It won't want an enthusiastic youngster running around under its feet all the time. Moreover, a puppy needs plenty of sleep and may have to have the brakes put on it once in a while.

The combination of a male and female needs special attention and it's good advice to get a second dog of the same sex. This will avoid a lot of problems. Sterilisation and castration is, of course, one solution, but it's a final one. A sterilised or castrated animal can never reproduce.

A dog and children

Dogs and children are a great combination. They can play together and get great pleasure out of each other's company. Moreover, children need to learn how to handle living beings; they develop respect and a sense of responsibility by caring for a dog (or other pets). However sweet a dog is, children must understand that it is an animal and not a toy. A dog isn't comfortable when it's being messed around with. It can become frightened, timid and even aggressive. So make it clear what a dog likes and what it doesn't. Look for ways the child can play with the dog, perhaps a game of hide-and-seek where the child hides and the dog has to find it. Even a simple tennis ball can give enormous pleasure. Children must learn to leave a dog in peace when it doesn't want to play any more. The dog must also have its own place where it's not disturbed. Have children help with your dog's care as much as possible. A strong bond will be the result.

The arrival of a baby also means changes in the life of a dog. Before the birth you can help get

the dog acquainted with the new situation. Let it sniff at the new things in the house and it will quickly accept them. When the baby has arrived, involve the dog as much as possible in day-by-day events, but make sure it gets plenty of attention too. NEVER leave a dog alone with young children. Crawling infants sometimes make unexpected movements, which can easily frighten a dog. And infants are hugely curious, and may try to find out whether the tail is really fastened to the dog, or whether its eyes come out, just like they do with their cuddly toys. But a dog is a dog and it will defend itself when it feels threatened.

Where to buy

There are various ways of acquiring a dog. The decision for a puppy or an adult dog will also define for the most part where to buy your dog.

If it's to be a puppy, then you need to find a breeder with a litter. If you chose a popular breed, like the Rottweiler, there is choice enough. But you may also face the problem that there are so many puppies on sale that have only been bred for profit's sake. You can see how many puppies are for sale by looking in the regional newspaper every Saturday. Some of these dogs have a pedigree, but many don't. These breeders often don't watch out for

breed-specific illnesses and in-breeding; puppies are separated from their mother as fast as possible and are thus insufficiently socialised. Never buy a puppy that is too young, or whose mother you weren't able to see.

Fortunately there are also enough bona-fide breeders of Rottweilers. Try to visit a number of breeders before you actually buy your puppy. Ask if the breeder is prepared to help you after you've bought your puppy, and to help you find solutions for any problems that may come up.

We recommend that you buy a Rottweiler via the breed clubs. Breeders that are members of the association must meet its breeding rules. Any breeder that does not stick to these strict conditions is expelled. Under these rules, the parent dogs must be examined for hip dysplasia and must also have undergone a behaviour test or alternatively have gained a certificate in safety in traffic conditions. Potential breeding animals should have been awarded a 'very good' score at least twice in a show. They must not be younger than 28 months and bitches must not be older than eight years and nine months. After the birth, the litter is checked by the breed association. Some breed associations also often have a puppy information service where

you can get information about puppies available within the association. They also help place adult dogs that can no longer be kept by their owners due to personal circumstances (divorce, moving home etc.).

Finally, you must also realise that a pedigree is nothing more or less than evidence of descent. The kennel clubs also award pedigree certificates to the offspring of parents suffering from hereditary defects, or that have not been examined for these. A pedigree says nothing about the health of the parents.

Things to watch out for

Buying a puppy is no simple matter. You must pay attention to the following:

• Never buy a puppy on impulse, even if it is love at first sight. A dog is a living being that will need care and attention over a long period. It is not a toy that you can put away when you're done with it.

• Take a good look at the mother. Is she calm, nervous, aggressive, well cared-for or neglected? The behaviour and condition of the mother is not only a sign of the quality of the breeder, but also of the puppy you're about to buy.

• Avoid buying a puppy whose mother has been kept only in a kennel. A young dog needs as many different impressions as possible in its first few months, including living in a family group. It gets used to people and possibly other pets. Kennel dogs miss these experiences and are inadequately socialised.

• Always ask to see the parents' papers (vaccination certificates, pedigrees, official reports on health examinations).

• Preferably, choose a puppy from parents that have successfully passed the breed association's behaviour test (read more about this on page 42).

• Never buy a puppy younger than eight weeks.

• Put all agreements with the breeder in writing. A model agreement is available from the breed association.

Ten golden puppy rules

1. Let your puppy outdoors in doses: one hour play, then a feed followed by three hours sleep.
2. Never let a puppy run endlessly after a ball or a stick.
3. Don't let your puppy romp with big, heavy dogs.
4. Don't let your puppy play on a full stomach.
5. Don't give your puppy anything to drink straight after its food.
6. Don't let your puppy go up and down stairs in its first year; be careful with smooth floors.
7. Don't add supplements to ready-made foods.
8. Watch your puppy's weight; being overweight can lead to bone deformities.
9. Give your puppy a quiet place to sleep.
10. Pick up your puppy carefully, one hand under its chest, the other under its hindquarters.

Travelling with your Rottweiler

There are a few things to think about before travelling with your dog. While one dog may enjoy travelling, another may hate it. You may like holidays in far-away places, but it's questionable whether your dog will enjoy them as much as you do.

That very first trip

The first trip of a puppy's life is also the most nerve-wrecking. This is the trip from the breeder's to its new home. If you can, pick up your puppy in the early morning. Then it will have plenty of time to get used to its new surroundings. Ask the breeder not to feed the puppy that day. The young animal will be overwhelmed by all kinds of new experiences. Firstly, it's away from its mother; it's in a small room (the car) with all its different smells, noises and strange people. So there's a big chance that the puppy will be car-sick this first time, with the annoying consequence that it will remember travelling in the car as an unpleasant experience. So it's important to make this first trip as pleasant as possible. When

picking up a puppy, always take someone with you who can sit in the back seat with the puppy on his or her lap and talk to it calmly. If it's too warm for the puppy, a place on the floor at the feet of your companion is ideal. The pup will lie there relatively quietly and may even take a nap. Ask the breeder for a cloth or something else from the puppies' basket or bed that carries a familiar scent. The puppy can lie on this in the car, and it will also help if it feels lonely during the first nights at home.

If the trip home is a long one, then stop for a break (once in a while). Let your puppy roam and sniff around (on the lead!), offer it a little drink and, if necessary, let it do its business. Do take care to lay an old towel in the car. It can happen that the puppy, in its nervousness, may urinate or be sick. It's also good advice to give a puppy positive experiences with car journeys. Make short trips to nice places where you can walk and play with it. It can be a real nuisance if your dog doesn't like travelling in a car. After all, once in a while you will have to take it to certain places, such as the vet's or to visit friends and acquaintances.

Taking your Rottweiler on holiday

When making holiday plans, you also need to think about what you're going to do with your dog during that time. Are you taking it with you, putting it into kennels or leaving it with friends? In any event there are a number of things you need to do in good time. If you want to take your dog with you, you need to be sure in advance that it will be welcome at your holiday home, and what rules there are.

If you're going abroad it will need certain vaccinations and a health certificate, which normally need to be done four weeks before departure. You must also be sure that you've made all the arrangements necessary to bring your dog back home to the UK, without it needing to go into quarantine under the rabies regulations. Your vet can give you the most recent information.

If your trip is to Southern Europe, ask for a treatment against ticks (you can read more about this in the chapter on Parasites).

Although dog-owners usually enjoy taking their dog on holiday, you must seriously ask yourself whether the dog feels that way too. Rottweilers certainly don't always feel comfortable in a hot country. Days spent travelling in a car are also often not their preference, and some dogs suffer badly from car-sickness. There are good medicines for this, but it's questionable whether you're doing your dog a favour with them. If you do decide to take it with you, make regular stops at safe places during your journey, so that your dog can have a good run. Take plenty of fresh drinking water

with you, as well as the food your dog is used to. Don't leave your dog in the car standing in the sun. It can quickly be overcome by the heat, with even fatal consequences. If you can't avoid it, park the car in the shade if at all possible, and leave a window open for a little fresh air. Even if you've taken these precautions, never stay away long!

If you're travelling by plane or ship, make sure in good time that your dog can travel with you and what rules you need to observe. You will need some time to make all the arrangements. Maybe you decide not to take your dog with you, and you then need to find somewhere for it to stay. Arrangements for a place in kennels need to be made well in advance, and there may be certain vaccinations required, which need to be given a minimum of one month before the stay.

If your dog can't be accommodated in the homes of relatives or friends, it might be possible to have an acquaintance stay in your house. This also needs to be arranged well in advance, as it may be difficult to find someone that can do this.

Always ensure that your dog can be traced should it run away or get lost while on holiday. A little tube with your address or a tag with home and holiday address can prevent a lot of problems.

Moving home

Dogs generally become more attached to humans than to the house they live in. Moving home is usually not a problem for them. But it can be useful before moving to let the dog get to know its new home and the area around it.

If you can, leave your dog with relatives or friends (or in kennels) on the day of the move. The chance of it running away or getting lost is then practically non-existent. When your move is complete, you can pick your dog up and let it quietly get familiar with its new home and environment. Give it its own place in the house at once and it will quickly adapt. During the first week or so, always walk your dog on a lead because an animal can also get lost in new surroundings. Always take a different route so it quickly gets to know the neighbourhood.

Don't forget to get your new address and phone number engraved on the dog's tag. Send a change of address notice to the chip or tattoo registration office. Dogs must sometimes be registered in a new community.

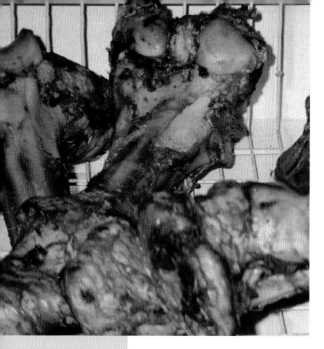

Feeding your Rottweiler

A dog will actually eat a lot more than just meat. In the wild it would eat its prey complete with skin and fur, including the bones, stomach, and the innards with their semi-digested vegetable material.

In this way the dog supplements its meat menu with the vitamins and minerals it needs. This is also the basis for feeding a domestic dog.

Ready-made foods

It's not easy for a layman to put together a complete menu for a dog, that includes all the necessary proteins, fats, vitamins and minerals in just the right proportions and quantities. Meat alone is certainly not a complete meal for a dog. It contains too little calcium. A calcium deficiency over time will lead to bone defects, and for a fast-growing puppy this can lead to serious skeletal deformities.

If you mix its food yourself, you can easily give your dog too much in terms of vitamins and minerals, which can also be bad for your dog's health. You can avoid these problems by giving it ready-made food of a good brand. These products are well-balanced and contain everything your dog needs. Supplements such as vitamin preparations are superfluous. The amount of food your dog needs depends on its weight and activity level. You can find guidelines on the packaging. Split the food into two meals per day if possible, and always ensure there's a bowl of fresh drinking water next to its food.

Give your dog the time to digest its food, don't let it outside straight after a meal. A dog should also never play on a full stomach. This can cause stomach torsion (the stomach turning over), which can be fatal for your dog.

Because the nutritional needs of a dog depend, among other things, on its age and way of life, there are many different types of dog food available. There are "light" foods for less active dogs, "energy" foods for working dogs and "senior" foods for the older dog.

Puppy chunks

There is now a wide assortment of puppy chunks on the market. These chunks contain a higher content of growth-promoting nutrients, such as protein and calcium. For large breeds such as the Rottweiler however, these chunks can actually be harmful. The dog will grow fast enough, and faster growth will only pro-mote conditions such as hip and elbow dysplasia (see the chapter Your Rottweiler's health). Give your puppy only special puppy chunks for larger breeds.

Canned foods, mixer and dry foods

Ready-made foods available at pet shops or in the supermarket can roughly be split into canned food, mixer and dry food. Whichever form you choose, ensure that it's a complete food with all the necessary ingredients. You can see this on the packaging.

Most dogs love canned food. Although the better brands are composed well, they do have one disadvantage: they are soft. A dog fed only on canned food will sooner or later have problems with its teeth (plaque, paradontosis). Besides canned food, give your dog hard foods at certain times or a dog chew, such as Nylabone Healthy Edibles.

Mixer is a food consisting of chunks, dried vegetables and grains. Almost all moisture has been extracted. The advantages of mixer are that it is light and keeps well. You add a certain amount of water and the meal is ready. A disadvantage is that it must definitely not be fed without water. Without the extra fluid, mixer will absorb the fluids present in the stomach, with serious results. Should your dog manage to get at the bag and enjoy its contents, you must immediately give it plenty to drink.

Dry chunks have also had the moisture extracted but not as much as mixer. The advantage of dry foods is that they are hard, forcing the dog to use its jaws, removing plaque and massaging the gums.

Dog chew products

Of course, once in a while you want to spoil your dog with some-thing extra. Don't give it pieces of cheese or sausage as these contain too much salt and fat. There are various products available that a dog will find delicious and which are also healthy, especially for its teeth. You'll find a large range of varying quality in the pet shop.

The butcher's left-overs

The bones of slaughtered animals have traditionally been given to the dog and dogs are crazy about them, but they are not without risks. Pork and poultry bones are too weak. They can splinter and cause serious injury to the intestines. Beef bones are more suitable, but they must first be cooked to kill off dangerous bacteria. Pet shops carry a range of smoked, cooked and dried abattoir residue, such as pigs' ears, bull penis, tripe sticks, oxtails, gullet, dried muscle meat, and hoof chews.

Fresh meat

If you do want to give your dog fresh meat occasionally, never give it raw, but always boiled or roasted. Raw (or not fully cooked) pork or chicken can contain life-threatening bacteria. Chicken can be contaminated by the notorious salmonella bacteria, while pork can carry the Aujeszky virus.

This disease is incurable and will quickly lead to the death of your pet.

Buffalo or cowhide chews
Dog chews are mostly made of beef or buffalo hide. Chews are usually knotted or pressed hide and can come in the form of little shoes, twisted sticks, lollies, balls and various other shapes; nice to look at and a nice change.

Munchy sticks
Munchy sticks are green, yellow, red or brown coloured sticks of various thicknesses. They consist of ground buffalo hide with a number of often undefined additives. The composition and quality of these between-meal treats is not always clear. Some are fine, but there have also been sticks found to contain high levels of cardboard and even paint residues. Choose a product whose ingredients are clearly described.

Something to drink
A dog can go days without eating if it must, but definitely not without drinking! Make sure it always has a bowl of fresh water available. Food and water bowls of stainless steel are the easiest to keep clean.

Overweight?
Recent investigations have shown that many dogs are overweight. A dog usually gets too fat because of over-feeding and lack of exercise. Use of medicines or a disease is

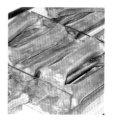

rarely the cause. Dogs that get too fat are often given too much food or treats between meals. Gluttony or boredom can also be a cause, and a dog often puts on weight following castration or sterilisation. Due to changes in hormone levels, it becomes less active and consumes less energy. Finally, simply too little exercise alone can lead to a dog becoming overweight.

You can use the following rule of thumb to check whether your dog is overweight: you should be able to feel its ribs, but not see them. If you can't feel its ribs then your dog is much too fat. Overweight dogs live a passive life, they play too little and tire quickly. They also suffer from all kinds of medical problems (problems in joints and heart conditions). They usually die younger too.

So it's important to make sure your dog doesn't get too fat. Always follow the guidelines on food packaging. Adapt them if your dog is less active or gets lots of snacks. Try to make sure your dog gets plenty of exercise by playing and running with it as much as you can. If your dog starts to show signs of putting on weight you can switch to a low-calorie food. If it's really too fat and reducing its food quantity doesn't help, then a special diet is the only solution.

Caring for your Rottweiler

Good (daily) care is extremely important for your dog. A well cared-for dog is less likely to become ill. Caring for your dog is not only necessary but also a pleasure.

Master and dog are giving each other some attention, and it's an excellent opportunity for a game and a cuddle.

The coat

Caring for your dog's coat involves regular brushing and combing, together with checking for parasites such as fleas. How often a dog needs to be brushed and combed depends on the length of its coat. Give your Rottweiler's coat a stiff brushing every day. Especially during the moulting period (twice a year), this is essential: brushing promotes the growth of the new coat and prevents your furniture becoming buried under dog's hairs. Brush in the direction the coat is growing, but also in the opposite direction. Keep brushing until no more loose hairs come out of the coat. Use the right equipment for taking care of the coat. Combs should not be too sharp and you should use a rubber or natural hairbrush.

If you get a puppy used to being brushed from an early age, it will enjoy having its coat cared for. Only bath a dog when it's really necessary. Always use a special dog shampoo and make sure it doesn't get into the dog's eyes or ears. Rinse the suds out thoroughly. Only let your dog outdoors again when it's completely dry. Even dogs can catch colds!

A vet can prescribe special medicinal shampoos for some skin conditions. Always follow the instructions to the letter.

Good flea prevention is highly important to avoid skin and coat problems. Fleas must be treated not only on the dog itself but also in its surroundings (see the chapter on Parasites). Coat problems can also occur due to an allergy to certain food substances. In such cases, a vet can prescribe a hypo-allergenic diet.

Teeth

A dog must be able to eat properly to stay in good condition, so it needs healthy teeth. Check its teeth regularly. Get in touch with your vet if you suspect that all is not well. Regular feeds of hard dry food can help keep your dog's teeth clean and healthy. There are special dog chews, such as Nylabone, on the market that help prevent plaque and help keep the animal's breath fresh. What really helps is to regularly brush your dog's teeth. You can use special toothbrushes for dogs, but a finger wrapped in a small piece of gauze will also do the job. Get your dog used to having its teeth cleaned at an early age and you won't have problems.

You can even teach an older dog to have its teeth cleaned. With a dog chew as a reward it will certainly be happy.

Nails

On a dog that regularly walks on hard surfaces, its nails usually grind themselves down. In this

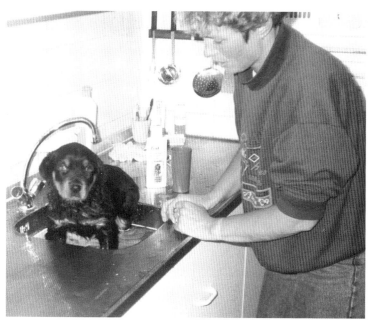

case there's no need to clip their nails. But it wouldn't do any harm to check their length now and again, especially on dogs that don't get out on the streets often. Using a piece of paper, you can easily see whether its nails are too long. If you can push the paper between the nail and the ground when the dog is standing, then the nail is the right length.

Nails that are too long can bother a dog. It can injure itself when scratching, so they must be kept trimmed. You can buy special nail clippers in pet shops. Be careful not to clip back too far as you could damage the skin around the nail, which can bleed profusely. If you feel unsure, have this necessary task done by a vet or a professional groomer.

Eyes

A dog's eyes should be cleaned regularly. Discharge gets into the corners of the eye. You can easily remove it by wiping it downward with your thumb. If you don't like doing that, use a piece of tissue or toilet paper.

Keeping your dog's eyes clean will take only a few seconds a day, so do it every day. If the discharge becomes yellow this could point to an irritation or infection. Eye drops (from your vet) will quickly solve this problem.

Ears

The ears are often forgotten when caring for dogs, but they must be checked at least once a week. If your dog's ears are very dirty or show too much wax, you must clean them. This should preferably be done with a clean cotton cloth, moistened with lukewarm water or baby oil. Cotton wool is not suitable due to the fluff it can leave behind. NEVER penetrate the ear canal with an object. If you do neglect cleaning your dog's ears there's a substantial risk of infection. A dog that is constantly scratching at its ears might be suffering from dirty ears, an ear infection or ear mites, making a visit to the vet essential.

Bringing up your Rottweiler

It is important that your dog is properly brought up and obedient. Not only will this bring you more pleasure, but it's also nicer for your environment.

This, of course, applies to every dog, but is particularly important for a large and powerful dog like the Rottweiler. With a badly brought-up Rottweiler you are asking for trouble!

A puppy can learn what it may and may not do by playing. Rewards and consistency are important tools in bringing up a dog. Reward it with your voice, a stroke or something tasty and it will quickly learn to obey. A puppy training course can also help you along the way.

(Dis)obedience
A dog that won't obey you is not just a problem for you, but also for your surroundings. It's therefore important to avoid unwanted behaviour. In fact, this

is what training your dog is all about, so get started early. 'Start 'em young!' applies to dogs too. An untrained dog is not just a nuisance, but can also cause dangerous situations by running into the road, chasing joggers or jumping at people. A dog must be trained out of this undesirable behaviour as quickly as possible. The longer you let it go on, the more difficult it will become to correct. The best thing to do is to attend a special obedience course. This won't only help to correct the dog's behaviour, but its owner also learns how to handle undesirable behaviour at home. A dog must not only obey its master during training, but at home too.

Always be consistent when training good behaviour and

correcting annoying behaviour. This means a dog may always behave in a certain way, or must never behave that way. Reward it for good behaviour and never punish it after the fact for any wrongdoing. If your dog finally comes after you've been calling it a long time, then reward it. If you're angry because you had to wait so long, it may feel it's actually being punished for coming. It will probably not obey at all the next time for fear of punishment.

Try to take no notice of undesirable behaviour. Your dog will perceive your reaction (even a negative one) as a reward for this behaviour. If you need to correct the dog, then do this immediately. Use your voice or grip it by the scruff of its neck and push it to the ground. This is the way a mother dog calls her pups to order. Rewards for good behaviour are, by far, preferable to punishment; they always get a better result.

House-training

The very first training (and one of the most important) that a dog needs is house-training. The basis for good house-training is keeping a good eye on your puppy. If you pay attention, you will notice that it will sniff a long time and turn around a certain spot before doing its business there. Pick it up gently and place it outside, always at the same place. Reward it abundantly if it does its business there.

Another good moment for house-training is after eating or sleeping. A puppy often needs to do its business at these times. Let it relieve itself before playing with it, otherwise it will forget to do so and you'll not reach your goal. For the first few days, take your puppy out for a walk just after it's eaten or woken up. It will quickly learn the meaning, especially if it's rewarded with a dog biscuit for a successful attempt.

Of course, it's not always possible to go out after every snack or snooze. Lay newspapers at different spots in the house. Whenever the pup needs to do its business, place it on a newspaper. After some time it will start to look for a place itself. Then start to reduce the number of newspapers until there is just one left, at the front or back door. The puppy will learn to go to the door if it needs to relieve itself. Then you put it on the lead and go out with it. Finally you can remove the last newspaper. Your puppy is now house-trained.

One thing that certainly won't work is punishing an accident after the fact. A dog whose nose is rubbed in its urine or its droppings won't understand that at all. It will only get frightened of you. Rewarding works much better than punishment. An indoor kennel or cage can be a good tool to help in house-training.

A puppy won't foul its own nest, so a kennel can be a good solution for the night, or during periods in the day when you can't watch it. But a kennel must not become a prison where your dog is locked up day and night.

First exercises

The basic commands for an obedient dog are those for sit, lie down, come and stay. But a puppy should first learn its name. Use it as much as possible from the first day on followed by a friendly 'Come!'. Reward it with your voice and a stroke when it comes to you. Your puppy will quickly recognise the intention and has now learned its first command in a playful manner. Don't be too harsh with a young puppy, and don't always punish it immediately if it doesn't always react in the right way. When you call your puppy to you in this way, have it come right to you. You can teach a pup to sit by holding a piece of dog biscuit above its nose and then slowly moving it backwards. The puppy's head will also move backwards until its hind legs slowly go down. At that moment you call 'Sit!'. After a few attempts, it will quickly know this nice game. Use the 'Sit!' command before you give your dog its food, put it on the lead, or before it's allowed to cross the street.

Teaching the command to lie down is similar. Instead of moving the piece of dog biscuit backwards, move it down vertically until your hand reaches the ground and then forwards. The dog will also move its forepaws forwards and lie down on its own. At that moment call 'Lie down!'. This command is useful when you want a dog to be quiet.

Two people are needed for the 'Come!' command. One holds the dog back while the other runs away. After about fifteen metres, he stops and enthusiastically calls 'Come!'. The other person now lets the dog go, and it should obey the command at once. Again you reward it abundantly. The 'Come!' command is useful in many situations and good for safety too.

A dog learns to stay from the sitting or lying position. While it's sitting or lying down, you give the command 'Stay!' and then step back one step. If the dog moves with you, quietly put it back in position, without displaying anger. If you do react angrily, you're actually punishing it for coming to you, and you'll only confuse your dog. It can't understand that coming is rewarded one time, and punished another. Once the dog stays nicely reward it abundantly. Practise this exercise with increasing distances (at first no more than one metre). The 'Stay!' command is useful when getting out of the car.

Courses

Because it is so important that a Rottweiler is properly brought up, we urgently recommend that you attend an obedience course with your dog. Obedience courses to help you bring up your dog are available across the country.

These courses are not just informative, but also fun for dog and master.

With a puppy, you can begin with a puppy course. This is designed to provide the basic training. A puppy that has attended such a course has learned about all kinds of things that will confront it in later life: other dogs, humans, traffic and what these mean. The puppy will also learn obedience and to follow a number of basic commands. Apart from all that, attention will be given to important subjects such as brushing, being alone, travelling in a car, and doing its business in the right places.

The next step after a puppy course is a course for young dogs. This course repeats the basic exercises and ensures that the growing dog doesn't get into bad habits. After this, the dog can move on to an obedience course for full-grown dogs. For more information on where to find courses in your area, contact your local kennel club. You can get its address from the Kennel Club of Great Britain in London. In some areas, the RSPCA organises obedience classes and your local branch may be able to give you information.

Play and toys
There are various ways to play with your dog. You can romp and run with it, but also play a number of games, such as retrieving, tug-of-war, hide-and-seek and catch. A tennis ball is ideal for retrieving, you can play tug-of-war with an old sock or a special tugging rope. Start with tug-of-war only when your dog is a year old. A puppy must first get its second teeth and then they need several months to strengthen. There's a real chance of your dog's teeth becoming deformed if you start too young. You can use almost anything for a game of hide-and-seek. A frisbee is ideal for catching games. Never use too small a ball for games. It can easily get lodged into the dog's throat.

Play is extremely important. Not only does it strengthen the bond between dog and master, but it's also healthy for both. Make sure that you're the one that ends the game. Only stop when the dog has brought back the ball or frisbee, and make sure you always win the tug-of-war. This confirms your dominant position in the hierarchy. Use these toys only during play so that the dog doesn't forget their significance. When choosing a special dog toy, remember that dogs are hardly careful with them. So always buy toys of good quality that a dog can't easily destroy.

Be very careful with sticks and twigs. The latter, particularly, can easily splinter. A splinter of wood in your dog's throat or intestines can cause awful problems.

Throwing sticks or twigs can also be dangerous. If they stick into the ground a dog can easily run into them with an open mouth.

If you would like to do more than just play games, you can now also play sports with your dog. For people who want to do more, there are various other sporting alternatives such as flyball, agility, obedience, guard-dog and tracking training.

Aggression

Rottweilers are working dogs and certainly need a portion of aggression to do their work (guarding and protection). A Rottweiler that lacks this normal aggression is no Rottweiler by nature. A responsibly bred and properly raised Rottweiler will apply its aggression (defence instinct) only in the moment that it actually needs to defend something. Sadly however, there are enough cases recorded where Rottweilers have given vent to their aggression at the wrong moment, in some cases even with fatal consequences.

These incidents have led to a broad discussion in society about Rottweilers and other breeds of dog with above average levels of aggression. Some governments are working on aggression tests for such breeds. By making such tests mandatory, it is hoped to track down excessively aggressive dogs before they can reproduce. Contact the breed association for more information on these tests.

Poor upbringing. One cannot overemphasise that a Rottweiler needs a rigorous and consistent upbringing with a strong hand. If this doesn't happen, there is a high risk that it will not be able to contain its aggression at a certain moment!

In general, there are two different types of aggressive behaviour: The anxious-aggressive dog and the dominant-aggressive dog. An anxious-aggressive dog can be recognised by its pulled back ears and its low position. It will have pulled in its lips, showing its teeth. This dog is aggressive because it's very frightened and feels cornered. It would prefer to run away, but if it can't then it will bite to defend itself. It will grab its victim anywhere it can. The attack is usually brief and, as soon as the dog can see a way to escape, it's gone. In a confrontation with other dogs, it will normally turn out as the loser. It can become even more aggressive once it's realised that people or other dogs are afraid of it. This behaviour cannot be corrected just like that. First you have to try and understand what the dog is afraid of. Professional advice is a good idea here because the wrong approach can easily make the problem worse.

Rottweilers are, in the main, dominant-aggressive dogs. The dominant-aggressive dog's body

Abnormal aggression in Rottweilers has two possible causes:

Poor breeding policy. Some breeders (outside the breed association) pay insufficient attention to the parent animals' characters when composing breeding pairs. The character of a dog, however, has been an important issue for the breed associations for many years. Over time, the associations have developed very suitable aggression tests for Rottweilers. One should actually only breed with animals that have passed this test successfully. Some associations also permit breeding with animals that have only passed a traffic safety test, but this is in fact not suitable as a test for aggression. If you can, buy only a puppy from parents that have passed the aggression test.

language is different. Its ears stand up and its tail is raised and stiff. This dog will always go for its victim's arms, legs or throat. It is extremely self-assured and highly placed in the dog hierarchy. Its attack is a display of power rather than a consequence of fear. This dog needs to know who's boss. You must bring it up rigorously and with a strong hand. An obedience course can help.

A dog may also bite itself because it's in pain. This is a natural defensive reaction. In this case try to resolve the dog's fear as far as possible. Reward it for letting you get to the painful spot. Be careful, because a dog in pain may also bite its master! Muzzling it can help prevent problems if you have to do something that may be painful. Never punish a dog for this type of aggression!

Fear

The source of anxious behaviour can often be traced to the first weeks of a dog's life. A shortage of new experiences during this important phase (also called the 'socialisation phase') has great influence on its later behaviour. A dog that never encountered humans, other dogs or animals during the socialisation phase will be afraid of them later. This fear is common in dogs brought up in a barn or kennel, with almost no contact with humans. As we saw, fear can lead to aggressive behaviour, so it's important that a puppy gets as many new impressions as possible in the first weeks of its life. Take it with you

into town in the car or on the bus, walk it down busy streets and allow it to have plenty of contact with people, other dogs and other animals.

It's a huge task to turn an anxious, poorly socialised dog into a real pet. It will probably take an enormous amount of attention, love, patience and energy to get such an animal used to everything around it. Reward it often and give it plenty of time to adapt and, over time, it will learn to trust you and become less anxious. Try not to force anything, because that will always have the reverse effect. Here too, an obedience course can help a lot. A dog can be especially afraid of strangers. Have visitors give it something tasty as a treat. Put a can of dog biscuits by the door so that your visitors can spoil your dog when they arrive. Here again, don't try to force anything. If the dog is still frightened, leave it in peace.

Dogs are often frightened in certain situations; well-known examples are thunderstorms and fireworks. In these cases try to ignore their anxious behaviour. If you react to a dog's whimpering and whining, it's the same as rewarding it. If you ignore its fear completely, your dog will quickly learn that nothing is wrong. You can speed up this 'learning process' by rewarding its positive behaviour.

Rewarding

Rewarding forms the basis for bringing up a dog. Rewarding good behaviour works far better than punishing bad behaviour and rewarding is also much more fun. Over time, the opinions on raising dogs have gradually changed. In the past the proper way to correct bad behaviour was regarded as a sharp pull on the lead. Today, experts view rewards as a positive incentive to get dogs to do what we expect of them. There are many ways to reward a dog. The usual ways are a stroke or a friendly word, even without a tasty treat to go with it. Of course, a piece of dog biscuit does wonders when you're training a puppy. Be sure you always have something delicious in your pocket to reward good behaviour. Another form of reward is play. Whenever a dog notices that you have a ball in your pocket, it won't go far from your side. As soon as you've finished playing, put the ball away. This way your dog will always do its best in exchange for a game.

Despite the emphasis you put on rewarding good behaviour, a dog can sometimes be a nuisance or disobedient. You must correct such behaviour immediately. Always be consistent: once 'no' must always be 'no'.

Barking

Dogs which bark too much and too often are a nuisance for their surroundings. A dog-owner may tolerate barking up to a point, but neighbours are often annoyed by the unnecessary noise. Don't encourage your puppy to bark and yelp. Of course, it should be able to announce its presence, but if it goes on barking it must be called to order with a strict 'Quiet!'. If a puppy fails to obey, just hold its muzzle closed with your hand.

A dog will sometimes bark for long periods when left alone. It feels threatened and tries to get someone's attention by barking. There are special training programmes for this problem, where dogs learn that being alone is nothing to be afraid of, and that their master will always return. You can practise this with your dog at home. Leave the room and come back in at once. Reward your dog if it stays quiet. Gradually increase the length of your absences and keep rewarding it as long as it remains quiet. Never punish the dog if it does bark or yelp. It will never understand punishment afterwards, and this will only make the problem worse. Never go back into the room as long as your dog is barking, as it will view this as a reward. You might want to make the dog feel more comfortable by switching the radio on for company during your absence. It will eventually learn that you always come back and the barking will reduce. If you don't get the required result, attend an obedience course.

Breeding

Dogs, and thus Rottweilers, follow their instincts, and reproduction is one of nature's important processes. For people who enjoy breeding dogs this is a positive circumstance.

Those who simply want a 'cosy companion' however, do not need the regular adventures with females on heat and unrestrainable males. Knowing a little about breeding in dogs will help you to understand why they behave the way they do, and the measures you need to take when this happens.

Liability

Breeding dogs is much more than simply 1+1= many. If you're planning to breed with your Rottweiler, be on your guard, otherwise the whole affair can turn into a financial drama because, under the law, a breeder is liable for the 'quality' of his puppies.

The breed clubs place strict conditions on animals used for breeding. They must be examined for possible congenital defects (see the chapter Your Rottweiler's health). This is the breeder's first obligation, and if you breed a litter and sell the puppies without these checks having been made, you can be held liable by the new owners for any costs arising from any inherited defects. These (veterinary) costs can be enormous! So contact the breed association if you plan to breed a litter of Rottweilers.

The female in season

Bitches become sexually mature at about eight to twelve months. Then they go into season for the first time. They are 'on heat' for two to three weeks. During this period they discharge little drops of blood and they are very attractive to males. The bitch is fertile during the second half of her season, and will accept a male to mate. The best time for mating is then between the ninth and thirteenth day of her season. A female's first season is often shorter and less severe than those that follow. If you do want to breed with your female you must allow this first (and sometimes the second) season to pass. Most bitches go into season twice per year.

If you do plan to breed with your Rottweiler in the future, then sterilisation is not an option to prevent unwanted offspring. A

temporary solution is a contraceptive injection, although this is controversial because of side effects such as womb infections.

Phantom pregnancy

A phantom pregnancy is a not uncommon occurrence. The female behaves as if she has a litter. She takes all kinds of things to her basket and treats them like puppies. Her teats swell and sometimes milk is actually produced. The female will sometimes behave aggressively towards people or other animals, as if she is defending her young. Phantom pregnancies usually begin two months after a season and can last a number of weeks.

If it happens to a bitch once, it will often then occur after every season. If she suffers under it, sterilisation is the best solution, because continual phantom pregnancies increase the risk of womb or teat conditions. In the short term a hormone treatment is worth trying, perhaps also homeopathic medicines. Camphor spirit can give relief when teats are heavily swollen, but rubbing the teats with ice or a cold cloth (moisten and freeze) can also help relieve the pain.

Feed the female less than usual, and make sure she gets enough attention and extra exercise.

Preparing to breed

If you do plan to breed a litter of puppies, you must first wait for your female to be physically and mentally full-grown. In any event you must let her first season pass. To mate a bitch, you need a male. You could simply let her out on the street and she will quickly return home pregnant.

But if you have a pure-bred Rottweiler, then it certainly makes sense to mate her with the best possible candidate, even if she has no pedigree. Proceed with caution and think especially about the following: Accompanying a bitch through pregnancy, birth and the first eight to twelve weeks afterwards is a time-consuming affair. Never breed with Rottweilers that have congenital

defects, and this also applies to dogs without papers. The same goes for hyperactive, nervous and shy dogs. If your Rottweiler bitch does have a pedigree, then mate her with a dog that also has one. For more information, contact the breed association.

Pregnancy

It's often difficult to tell at first when a bitch is pregnant. Only after about four weeks can you feel the pups in her womb. She will now slowly get fatter and her behaviour will usually change. Her teats will swell during the last few weeks of pregnancy. The average pregnancy lasts 63 days, and costs her a lot of energy. In the beginning she is fed her normal amount of food, but her nutritional needs increase in jumps during the second half of the pregnancy. Give her approximately fifteen percent more food each week from the fifth week on. The mother-to-be needs extra energy and proteins during this phase of her pregnancy.

During the last weeks you can give her a concentrated food, rich in energy, such as dry puppy food. Divide this into several small portions per day, because she can no longer deal with large portions of food. Towards the end of the pregnancy, her energy needs can easily be one-and-a-half times more than usual.

After about seven weeks the mother will start to demonstrate nesting behaviour and to look for a place to give birth to her young. This might be her own basket or a special birthing box. This must be ready at least a week before the birth to give the mother time to get used to it. The basket or box should preferably be in a quiet place.

The birth

The average litter is between three and nine puppies. The birth usually passes without problems. Of course, you must contact your vet immediately if you suspect a problem!

Suckling

After birth, the mother starts to produce milk. The suckling period is very demanding. During the first three to four weeks the pups rely entirely on their mother's milk. During this time she needs extra food and fluids. This can be up to three or four times the normal amount. If she's producing too little milk, you can give both mother and her young special puppy milk. Here too, divide the high quantity of food the mother needs over several smaller portions. Again, choose a concentrated, high-energy, food and give her plenty of fresh drinking water, but not cow's milk, which can cause diarrhoea.

You can give the puppies some supplemental solid food when they are three to four weeks old. There are special puppy foods available that follow on well from the mother's milk and can easily be eaten with their milk teeth.

Ideally, the puppies are fully weaned at an age of six or seven weeks, i.e. they no longer drink their mother's milk. The mother's milk production gradually stops and her food needs also drop. Within a couple of weeks after weaning, the mother should again be getting the same amount of food as before the pregnancy.

Castration and sterilisation

As soon as you are sure your bitch should never bear a (new) litter, a vasectomy or sterilisation is the best solution. During sterilisation (in fact this is normal castration) the uterus is removed in an operation. The bitch no longer goes into season and can never become pregnant. The best age for a sterilisation is about eighteen months, when the bitch is more or less fully grown.

A male dog is usually only castrated for medical reasons or to correct undesirable sexual behaviour. During a castration the testicles are removed, which is a simple procedure and usually without complications. There is no special age for castration but, where possible, wait until the dog is fully grown. Vasectomy is sufficient where it's only a case of making the dog infertile. In this case the dog keeps its sexual drive but can no longer reproduce.

Sports and shows

The Rottweiler is a working dog through and through. The breed has been developed to work, and that's the way it should stay. Naturally, many people enjoy taking their Rottweilers to dog shows.

However care needs to be taken in breeding so that the breed's characteristics do not become adapted to show requirements.

Anyone that buys a Rottweiler must realise that this is not a lap dog. A working dog wants to work and must be allowed to do so. Without sufficient work and exercise, it will become frustrated, bored and fat. A Rottweiler that has something to do will exploit its character and energy in a positive manner.

Rottweilers do not learn as quickly as some other breeds. They need lots of repetition. Therefore, more patience is needed in training a Rottweiler than with a German Shepherd for example. Furthermore, it

thoroughly enjoys training and during work a strong bond between master and dog will develop.

Guard dog training
In principle, a Rottweiler can perform various tasks, but by nature it is a true guard dog. Guard work is a serious element of dog sports. This training consists of three elements: tracking, obedience and guard work (arrest work). Guard dog training is a difficult course that places high demands on dog and master. The guard work portion is spectacular. However, a dog must be totally obedient before you can train it. People often think that arrest training makes a dog spiteful and untrustworthy, but the opposite is true. During guard

service a dog must be extremely controlled, disciplined and easy to handle, and for this reason there are high demands in terms of obedience for guard service.

Tracker dog training

The Rottweiler is also a very talented tracker dog. Although it may not appear difficult at first sight, tracking is hard and intensive work for a dog. The dog must display sure tracking abilities and track a scent that is 1½ miles long and at least three hours old. There are seven turns in the scent (matching the terrain). The trace is crossed by two distracting scents a good distance from each other. There are also seven objects at varying distances on the track.

Exhibitions and exemption shows

Visiting a dog show is a pleasant experience for both dog and master, and for some dog-lovers it is an intensive hobby. They visit countless shows every year. Others find it nice to visit an exemption show with their dog just once. It's worth making the effort to visit an exemption show where a judge's experienced eyes will inspect your Rottweiler and assess it for form, gait, condition and behaviour. The judge's report will teach you your dog's weak and strong points, which may help you when choosing a mate for breeding. You can also exchange experiences with other Rottweiler owners. Official dog shows are only open to dogs with a pedigree.

Ring training

If you've never been to a dog show, you will probably be fumbling in the dark in terms of what will be expected of you and your dog. Many kennel clubs organise so-called ring training courses for dogs going to a show for the first time. This training teaches you exactly what the judge will be looking for, and you can practice this together with your dog.

Open shows

Almost all kennel clubs organise dog shows. You must register your dog in advance in a certain class. These meetings are usually small and friendly and are often the first acquaintance dog and master make with a judge. This is an overwhelming experience for your dog - a lot of its contemporaries and a strange man or woman who fiddles around with it and peers into its mouth. After a few times, your dog will know exactly what's expected of it and will happily go to the next club match.

Championship shows

Various championship shows take place during the course of the year with different prizes. These shows are much more strictly organised than club matches. Your dog must be registered in a certain class in advance and it will then be listed in a catalogue. On the day itself, the dog is usually kept on a bench until its turn comes up. During the judging in the ring, it's important that you show your dog at its best.

Don't forget!
If you're planning to take your dog
to a club match or in fact to any
show, you need to be well prepared.
Don't forget the following:

For yourself:
- Show documents if they have
  been sent to you
- Food and drink
- Clip for the catalogue number
- Chairs if an outside show

For your dog:
- Food and drink bowls and food
- Dog blanket and perhaps a cushion
- Show lead
- A brush
- A benching chain and collar

The judge examines each dog in
turn. When all the dogs from that
class have been judged, the best
are selected and placed. After the
judging has finished, all the
winners of the same sex in the
various classes compete for the
Challenge Certificate (3 Challenge
certificates from different judges,
and your Rottweiler will be a
Champion in the UK). The best
Rottweiler in the eyes of the judge
gets this award. Finally, the
winners of each sex compete for
the title of Best in Show.
Of course, your dog must look
very smart for the show. The
judge will not be impressed if its
coat is not clean and its paws are
dirty. Nails must be clipped and
teeth free of plaque.

The dog must also be free of
parasites and ailments. A bitch
must not be in season and a male
must be in possession of both
testicles. Apart from those things,
judges also hate badly brought-up,
anxious or nervous dogs. Get in
touch with your local dog club or
the breed association if you want
to know more about shows.

the **Rottweiler**

Parasites

All dogs are vulnerable to various sorts of parasite. Parasites are tiny creatures that live at the expense of another animal. They feed on blood, skin and other body substances. There are two main types.

Internal parasites live within their host animal's body (tapeworm and round-worm) and external parasites live on the animal's exterior, usually in its coat (fleas and ticks), but also in its ears (ear mite).

Fleas

Fleas feed on a dog's blood. They cause not only itching and skin problems, but can also carry infections such as tapeworm. In large numbers they can cause anaemia and dogs can also become allergic to a flea's saliva, which can cause serious skin conditions. So it's important to treat your dog for fleas as effectively as possible, not just on the dog itself but also in its surroundings. For treatment on the animal, there are various medicines: drops for the neck and to put in its food, flea collars, long-life sprays and flea powders.

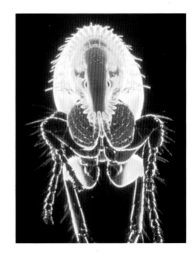

There are various sprays in pet shops that can be used to eradicate fleas in the dog's immediate surroundings. Choose a spray that kills both adult fleas and their larvae. If your dog goes in your car, you should spray that too.

Fleas can also affect other pets, so you should treat those too. When spraying a room, cover any aquarium or fishbowl. If the spray reaches the water, it can be fatal for your fish!

Your vet and pet shop have a wide range of flea treatments and can advise you on the subject.

Ticks

Ticks are small, spider-like parasites. They feed on the blood of the animal or person they've settled on. A tick looks like a tiny, grey-coloured leather bag with eight feet. When it has sucked itself full, it can easily be five to ten times its own size and is darker in colour.

Dogs usually fall victim to ticks in bushes, woods or long grass. Ticks cause not only irritation by their blood-sucking but can also carry a number of serious diseases. This applies especially to the Mediterranean countries, which can be infested with blood parasites. In our country these diseases are fortunately less common. But Lyme disease, which can also affect humans, has reached our shores. Your vet can prescribe a special treatment if you're planning to take your dog to Southern Europe. It is important to fight ticks as effectively as possible. Check your dog regularly, especially when it's been running free in woods and bushes. It can also wear an anti-tick collar.

Removing a tick is simple using a tick pincette. Grip the tick with the pincette as close to the dog's skin as possible and carefully pull it out. You can also grip the tick between your fingers and, using a turning movement, pull it carefully out. You must disinfect the spot where the tick was using iodine to prevent infection. Never soak the tick in alcohol, ether or oil. In a shock reaction the tick may discharge the infected contents of its stomach into the dog's skin.

Worms

Dogs can suffer from various types of worm. The most common are tapeworm and roundworm. Tapeworm causes diarrhoea and poor condition. With a tapeworm infection you can sometimes find small pieces of the worm around the dog's anus or on its bed. In this case, the dog must be wormed. You should also check your dog for fleas, which carry the tapeworm infection. Roundworm is a condition that reoccurs regularly. Puppies are often infected by their mother's milk. Your vet has medicines to prevent this. Roundworm causes problems (particularly in younger dogs), such as diarrhoea, loss of weight and stagnated growth. In serious cases the pup becomes thin, but with a swollen belly. It may vomit and you can then see the worms in its vomit. They are spaghetti-like tendrils. A puppy must be treated regularly for worms with a worm treatment. Adult dogs should be treated every six months.

Ticks

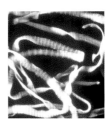

Tapeworms

Roundworms

Your Rottweiler's health

The space in this book is too limited to go into the medical ups and downs of the Rottweiler. But we do want to give some brief information about ailments and disorders that affect this race more than other dogs.

Hip Dysplasia (HD)

Hip Dysplasia has long been a serious problem among the Rottweiler population. At one time, it appeared that even half of all dogs examined were suffering from a serious form of HD. Thanks to a strict breeding policy imposed by the breed association, this percentage has now been drastically reduced.

Hip Dysplasia is an abnormality of the hip joints in the hind quarters, whereby the socket of the hip joint and the head of the upper thigh don't match properly. This causes inflammation and bone tumours, which can be very painful. Until recently, it was assumed that HD was primarily caused by genetic factors. Recent investigations, however, indicate that while genetic factors certainly play a role in terms of a dog's susceptibility to HD, external factors such as food quality and exercise appear at least equally important. Limit the chance of HD as far as possible by giving your dog ready-made food of a good brand, and don't add any supplements! Make sure your dog doesn't get too fat. A Rottweiler pup must be somewhat protected from HD in its first year. Don't let your puppy romp too much with other dogs or chase sticks and balls too wildly. These kinds of games cause the pup to make abrupt and risky movements, which can overburden its soft joints. One important but under-estimated factor behind HD is the floor in your home. Parquet and tiled floors are much too slippery for a young dog. Regular slipping can cause complications that promote HD. If you have a smooth floor, it's advisable to lay blankets or old carpet in places the dog uses regularly. Let it spend lots of time in the garden, as grass is a perfect surface to run on.

Elbow Dysplasia (ED)

Elbow Dysplasia generally appears during the first year of a puppy's life. This condition is similar to HD, but affects the forelegs. In the worst case ED can cause lameness. An operation is then needed, which is usually successful. The measures you can take to reduce the chance of ED are the same as for HD.

Entropion and ectropion

These are genetic conditions affecting the eyelids. With entropion the eyelids are curled inwards, with ectropion outwards. Both cause the eyelashes to lay on the eyeball causing irritation, which leads to red, watering eyes. The eyes become infected and discharge pus. This can cause serious damage to the cornea and eventually even cause blindness. Entropion and ectropion can be corrected surgically.

Tips for the Rottweiler

- If you can, buy a puppy from parents that have passed a behaviour test.
- Don't let your puppy romp with large, heavy dogs.
- A Rottweiler needs a master or mistress with authority!
- Don't only fight fleas, but also their larvae.
- Don't let your puppy run up and down stairs in its first six months.

- Follow a puppy course with your dog. You will both benefit.
- Buy your puppy from a reliable breeder.
- It is important that your dog feels comfortable in the car.
- If you can, buy a Rottweiler via the breed association.
- Reward works better than punishment when raising a dog.
- Protect your dog against ticks: they can cause dangerous illnesses!
- Hard chunks and plenty to chew on promote healthy teeth.
- Only give a Rottweiler puppy chunks for larger breeds.
- Visit various breeders before buying a puppy.
- A badly raised Rottweiler is asking for trouble.

The Rottweiler on the Internet

A great deal of information can be found on the internet. A selection of websites with interesting details and links to other sites and pages is listed here. Sometimes pages move to another site or address. You can find more sites by using the available search-machines.

www.rottweiler.co.uk
A dedicated & comprehensive web site for all Rottweiler enthusiasts.

www.britishrottweiler.co.uk
The British Rottweiler Association is dedicated to promoting good and responsible ownership, which is vital for a happy healthy life with your Rottweiler.

www.therottweilerclub.co.uk
The Rottweiler Club, the first specialist club for the breed, was formed in 1960. Their aim is to promote the well-being and public image of the breed now and for the future.

www.thescottishrottweiler-club.co.uk
The official Kennel Club recognized Breed Club in Scotland dedicated to the well-being of Rottweilers and owners throughout the U.K.

www.the-kennel-club.org.uk
The Kennel Club's primary objective is to promote, in every way, the general improvement of dogs. This site aims to provide you with information you may need to be a responsible pet owner and to help you keep your dog happy, safe and content.

www.k9-care.co.uk
The Self-Help site for dog owners. A beautiful website with tons of information on dogs. All you need to know about grooming, training, health care, buying a dog, travel and much more.

www.pet-insurance-uk.me.uk
Find low cost pet insurance via this UK pet insurance directory.

www.pethealthcare.co.uk
At PEThealthcare.co.uk they believe that a healthy pet is a happy pet. Which is why they've brought together leading experts to create a comprehensive online source of pet care information.

www.onlinepetcare.co.uk
www.onlinepetcare.co.uk was launched in 2001 and contains information about and links to businesses and charities in the Midlands area involved in the care and purchasing of domestic animals.

Breeders' Clubs

Becoming a member of a breeders' club can be very useful for good advice and interesting activities. Contact the Kennel Club in case addresses or telephone numbers have changed.

British Rottweiler Assoc.
Sec. Mrs M Yates
Tel: 01403 253228
http://www.britishrottweiler.co.uk/
Email:nicky@britishrottweiler.co.uk

Astern Counties Rottweiler Club
Sec. Mrs A E Fletcher
Tel: 01773 832522

London & South East Rottweiler Club
Sec. Mrs Davison
Tel: 020 8595 1826

Midland Rottweiler Club
Sec. Mrs J Blunden
Tel: 01773 590126

Northern Ireland Rottweiler Club
Sec. Ms McClay
Tel: 07790 040262

Northern Rottweiler Club
Sec. Mrs P Hammond
Tel: 01422 376984

Rottweiler Club
Sec. Miss David
Tel: 020 7737 5538

Rottweiler Club of Wales
Sec. Mr Lewis
Tel: 01443 674103

About Pets

Key features of the series are:

- Most affordable books
- Packed with hands-on information
- Well written by experts
- Easy to understand language
- Full colour original photography
- 70 to 110 photos
- All one needs to know to care well for one's pet
- Trusted authors, veterinary consultants, breed and species expert authorities
- Appropriate for first time pet owners
- Interesting detailed information for pet professionals
- Title range includes books for advanced pet owners and breeders
- Includes useful addresses, veterinary data, breed standards.

The Rottweiler

Name:	Rottweiler
F.C.I.-classification:	Pinscher and Schnauzer types, Molossian and Swiss mountain-& cattle-dogs (group II)
First standard:	approx. 1909
Origin:	Germany (Rottweil)
Original tasks:	Herding and guard dog
Shoulder height :	male: 60-68 cm (24 – 27 inches)
	bitch: 55-63 cm (22 – 25 inches)
Weight:	male: approx. 45-55 kg (100 – 120 lbs.)
	bitch: approx. 35-40 kg (75 – 90 lbs.)
Average life expectancy:	8-10 years